AF255879

The Gift

Matt McCarty

The Gift

Published in the United States of America

ISBN: 978-0-9863242-9-1

Library of Congress Catalog Card Number: 2014900047

Acknowledgements

I would like to thank my wife Mia for always believing in me during the process of writing this book. Thanks for sharing in the vision and for never failing to be my number one fan. Thanks for your insight, critiques, and genuine honesty along the way.
I love you.

Next, I want to thank my mother for encouraging me to chase my dreams. You taught me to do great things despite any obstacle that might come my way.
I love you too.

Finally, I want to thank Hannah Spangler for illustrating this book. You are truly a gifted illustrator and it was an honor of mine to have worked with you. Your professional career has a very bright future. Thanks for bringing life to my story.
I think you're pretty cool.

Dedication

This is for you, Dad. Thanks for teaching me to honor those who have bravely served our country.

This book is dedicated to you and every man or woman who has ever fought for our freedoms.

Dad, Rick, and Bill, thank you for your service.

It was Matthew's 10th birthday and he was excited to open his gifts. There were more gifts on the table than he had ever seen before! He and his friends sat around the table as he tore into them one by one.

He got a bunch of cool gifts that day. He got baseball cards, a new football, and even a powerful dart gun! But there was one thing he wanted most.

He wanted a new football video game called *Super Duper All Star Football*. All his friends had the game and they played it every day. He was so good at the game that he couldn't be defeated.

There was one gift left on the table from his mom and dad
and he knew it just had to be the video game.

He opened the package as fast as he could by ripping and tearing
the wrapping paper. He tossed the paper aside with so much joy
and excitement.

It was like a tornado of wrapping paper had just
blown through the kitchen!

Matthew wasn't sure what he had just opened. It didn't look like anything he had ever seen before. One thing was certain, it wasn't *Super Duper All Star Football*.

As he touched the gift it felt like the block letters he used to play with when he was in kindergarten. It was made of wood and stretched out as long as his own arm! As he turned it over it appeared to be a gigantic word.

"Freedom," he said as he read it out loud. "What's this mean dad? What's it for? Is my real gift inside these letters?" Matthew asked.

FREEDOM

FREEDOM

"Gather around boys.
I want to explain what this gift is all about," Dad said.

He began to explain that a boy's 10th birthday is a pretty big
deal and that it was time for them to learn a very important
lesson. Matthew's mom and sister joined them to hear
what Dad had to say.

"Boys," Dad began, "what we have here in front
of us is one of the greatest gifts a person can get.
I'm talking about the gift of freedom."

Dad then explained what freedom is. "Freedom means a person can do what they want to do, say what they want to say, and believe what they want to believe."

He told them that not everyone in the world has this gift and that freedom has a price.

"Just like you have to pay for toys or candy at the store, freedom has a price," Dad said. "Let me tell you a story about a man who paid a price so we could have freedom."

"Many years ago a very mean and angry man in Germany began taking away freedom from people. He was so mean, he put kids who hadn't done anything wrong in jail," Dad said.

"Kids couldn't go to school or play with their friends. They had to leave their mom and dad and live far away from them. This angry man made people burn books instead of reading them."

"He didn't let people do what they wanted to do, say what they wanted to say, or believe what they wanted to believe."

"People in America knew about freedom and knew that what the mean man was doing was wrong," his father explained.

"America sent many very brave men to Germany to save them. They jumped out of airplanes to surprise the angry man and to fight against him."

"A man named Captain Winters was one of the leaders who jumped out of a plane to save the kids in Germany. He was very brave and faced many dangers so that all of the people in Germany could have freedom."

"Captain Winters and his men won and the kids in Germany went back to school! The kids saw their moms and dads again and went back to reading books instead of burning them."

The kids and all of the people in Germany could once again do what they wanted to do, say what they wanted to say, and believe what they wanted to believe.

"I have a question," said Matthew's friend, Chad.

"What is it Chad?" Dad asked.

"What do you mean by paying the price?" he asked.

"That's a good question Chad!
People don't always pay money for things.
Sometimes they pay with their time or energy," said Dad.

"Do you mean like when I rake the leaves?" asked Matthew.

"You got it son!" Dad replied. "In order to rake the leaves you have to pay the price of time and energy. You'd rather play video games Saturday morning but you rake the leaves because it needs to get done."

"You see Matthew, freedom is a gift. Mom and I gave you this wooden gift so you will know how amazing freedom is."

"We also want you to know that you enjoy this gift
by being grateful," Dad continued.

Right away Chad's arm shot up into the air again!
"What does grateful mean?" Chad asked.

"Boy, Chad," Dad said as he laughed,
"you ask all of the right questions!"

"Grateful means that you enjoy a gift by thanking the one
who gave it to you. That's what we want you to do Matthew.
We want you to thank people like Captain Winters."

FREEDOM

Matthew thought long and hard about what
his father taught him and his friends that day.
It was the coolest birthday he'd ever had.

He went to bed that night forgetting he even wanted
a football video game.

Many years later, Matthew grew up into an adult with kids of his own. He had a very special job where he went to schools all across America to talk to kids about a very special gift. He was in airports a lot since he traveled so much.

One day he was waiting for a plane when he saw an old man sitting across from him in the airport. The man had a ball cap on his head that Matthew had seen before.

WORLD WAR II
VETERAN

WORLD
VET

Matthew knew just what he had to do.
He put his book down, got up, and walked right up to the man.

He looked him right in the eye, smiled, and said,
"Thank you, sir."

The old man looked confused at first and asked,
"What are you thanking me for?"

"I'm thanking you for paying the price, sir," Matthew answered.

With a tear running down his cheek the old man whispered,
"It was nothing. I did what I had to do."

"It was everything, sir," Matthew replied. "It was freedom.
Thanks for giving me one of the greatest gifts I've ever enjoyed."

Later that day Matthew could be heard speaking
to a group of kids in their classroom.

He said, "Remember, boys and girls, freedom isn't free.
Freedom costs time, energy, and sometimes even more
from men and women you see every day. Enjoy this gift by
thanking someone who paid the price for you."

The end.

FREEDOM

About the Author

Freedom was one of the many things Matt's father taught him about as a boy. He was taught that America was unique and special because it was designed in a way that made every man, woman, and child free. Matt also learned to honor those who purchased this great gift, and those who fight to defend it every single day. He was taught to express his gratitude by thanking an American veteran every single time he encountered one. Freedom is one of the greatest gifts that has been given to mankind and the men and women of America's Armed Services have purchased that gift at a great price.

Matt and his wife Mia founded McCarty Ministries, which was created to reach youth and train youth pastors and leaders all over America. They spend much of their time investing in the lives of America's youth, and have a heart to reach people with the message of faith. Matt is the author of numerous kid's books that teach American history and values. Matt also serves the men and women of the U.S. Armed Forces as a Supply Management Specialist with The Department of Defense, and is honored to assist them as they defend freedom. Matt earned his B.S. in Business Administration from Cornerstone University, his M.B.A. from Liberty University, and is a graduate of RHEMA Bible Training College in Tulsa Oklahoma. Matt and Mia live in Michigan with their children.

About the Illustrator

Hannah is a digital illustrator and animator specializing in portraits, character design, and concept art. She has animated award-winning short films, illustrated children's books, spoken at events, shown in galleries, and freelanced for over eight years working on projects such as the animated shorts *Overcomer* and *The Land Below*. She is currently based in Broken Arrow, Oklahoma where she continues to freelance and create original content. See more by visiting hannahgraceart.com.

www.ingramcontent.com/pod-product-compliance
Lightning Source LLC
Chambersburg PA
CBHW042204030726
47602CB00008B/125